LORD,

YOU CALLED

ME

Other Books by Ricardo Grzona

God With Us: The Story of Jesus
as Told by Matthew, Mark, Luke, and John

LORD, YOU CALLED ME

DISCERNING YOUR PATH IN LIFE

RICARDO GRZONA, FRP

LOYOLA PRESS.
A JESUIT MINISTRY
Chicago

LOYOLA PRESS.
A JESUIT MINISTRY

3441 N. Ashland Avenue
Chicago, Illinois 60657
(800) 621-1008
www.loyolapress.com

Comments and suggestions: Fundación Ramón Pané, cristonautas@cristonautas.com

Acknowledgements: Pope Francis I, who was the director of the Spiritual Exercises from which these reflections are taken

The Scripture quotations contained herein are from the *New Revised Standard Version Bible*, copyright ©1989 by the division of Christian Education of the National Council of the Churches of Christ in the U.S.A., and are used by permission. All rights reserved.

Cover Design: Loyola Press.
Cover art credit: Ink Drop/Shutterstock.com, aleksandarvelasevic/DigitalVision/Getty Images.
Illustrations: Kathryn Seckman Kirsch.

ISBN: 978-0-8294-5005-7
Library of Congress Control Number: 2019956551

Printed in the United States of America.
20 21 22 23 24 25 26 27 28 29 Versa 10 9 8 7 6 5 4 3 2 1

To Pope Francis, my spiritual director of many years, who guided me with wisdom and patience in my youth, and helped me discern my vocation to the service of spirituality.

CONTENTS

FOREWORD

FIAT VOLUNTAS TUA

The Ramón Pané Foundation and Brother Ricardo Grzona, F.R.P., offer *Lord, You Called Me: Discerning Your Path in Life* to those who wish to have an encounter with the Lord through his word, and through reading the Scriptures prayerfully, meditating on them, contemplating them, and bringing them into one's life—that is, following the methodology of *lectio divina*.

This book started as a pedagogical tool; it includes the notes that the author, Bro. Ricardo Grzona, made during his Spiritual Exercises when he was between nineteen and twenty-four years old under the direction of Fr. Jorge Bergoglio, SJ, now Pope Francis I. In these twenty-one chapters, or "encounters," Grzona develops a "holy reading," with texts from the Scriptures that recount God's calling of some biblical figures, beginning with Abraham; then with other figures of the Old Testament, Jacob, Joseph, Moses, Joshua, Samuel, and David; some of the prophets, Isaiah, Jeremiah, and Ezekiel; and arriving at the New Testament, where he focuses on the God's call of Mary, then of Matthew and the first disciples, and finally with the call to Paul.

Through their responses to their callings, these witnesses help us to grow in our generous response to the call that God the Father makes to each one of us, his children, so that in feeling the joy of encountering his son, Jesus Christ, we become his disciples and share with others the happiness and joy of following him. In this way, each chapter of the book helps the reader accept the role of missionary disciple and to further develop that role using the Scriptures by bringing them to life through contemplative action. Some of the values that this text touches on are faith, gratitude, trust, conversion, leadership, service, enthusiasm, self-confidence, freedom, forgiveness, and discipleship.

This material will be very useful to young people and those who guide them, particularly in light of the 2018 Synod that Pope Francis dedicated to "Young People, Faith, and Vocational Discernment." The introductory letter to the Synod reads: "By listening to young people, the Church will once again hear the Lord speaking in today's world. As in the days of Samuel (cf. 1 Sam 3:1–21) and Jeremiah (cf. Jer 1:4–10), young people know how to discern the signs of our times, indicated by the Spirit. Listening to their aspirations, the Church can glimpse the world which lies ahead and the paths the Church is called to follow."

I hope that this material will become a resource for contemplative prayer with the Scriptures for everyone, but especially for young people, so that on their way to Christian maturity they may discover, through guidance and discernment, the project that God has planned for their lives, and they will be prepared to carry it out with joy and generous self-giving, by serving the church and society.

Jorge Carlos Patrón Wong
Archbishop Emeritus of the Diocese of Papantla
Secretary for Seminaries of the Congregation for the Clergy
Vatican City

INTRODUCTION

Lord, you called me
to be an instrument of your grace,
to announce the good news,
to heal the souls.
Instrument of peace and of justice,
herald of all of your words,
water to calm the piercing thirst,
hand that blesses and loves.

Lord, you called me
to heal the wounded hearts,
to cry in the marketplace,
that Love is alive,
awaken those who slumber
and liberate the captured.
I am soft wax between your fingers,
do with me according to your will.

Lord, you called me
to save a tired world,
to love the people
that you, Father, gave me as brothers,
to alleviate misery and sin;
to make the stones tremble
and chase the wolves from the flock.
Amen.

The prayer on the previous page, which we recite during the morning prayer on Thursday during the second week of the Liturgy of the Hours, summarizes the reason for the title of these reflections, "*Lord, You Called Me.*"

The Lord calls and continues to call us. Throughout the Scriptures we find a persistent theme: When the people of God, or the community of the church, have concrete needs, God calls on us, humans, so that in his name we can offer guidance and act toward solutions. In a vocation, or call, everything is tangible: The need, God's help or resolution, and the person he chooses to bring about this resolution. This process continues as a kind of "established pattern."

Through these pages, you are invited to get to know the ways in which God revealed himself through his calls and actions in salvation history and also through the reactions of the people whom God called. Some doubted, others thought their abilities were inadequate, and others rebelled. Some who were called had very difficult pasts—they were sinners, they were distant from God, or they did not always feel competent. At first, almost every one of them rejected the call, but in the end, God prevailed, and they accepted their calling despite their imperfections and sin, allowing God to act through their actions. Through their example we can see God's greatness and mercy: "He came to call sinners, not the righteous."

In this book, you will find reflections on some of the calls that are recorded in the Scriptures. These reflections are taken from a notebook I kept during the Spiritual Exercises that I completed over several years. Fr. Jorge Mario Bergoglio, SJ, now Pope Francis I, was my spiritual director, and he guided me through my vocational discernment.

I later put these exercises together in the format of *lectio divina* to help provide a systematic way of understanding what happened in previous calls God made to key figures in the Bible, and to understand the way in which God calls each of us today. He calls us to continue to be the builders and writers of his plan for our Salvation. In other words, God fulfills his plan through us continuously.

I hope you will be able to identify with these biblical figures and discover that you, too, are called by God to be an instrument of his grace.

In reading this book, you may choose to challenge yourself to twenty-one days of reflections, or do them on an ongoing basis, as time allows. You can complete the *lectio divina* steps on your own or with your faith community. This book can also be used as a source for youth retreats with the guidance of a spiritual director.

I hope this book brings many blessings into your life as you begin this time of reflection, and that through it, God will help you discover your place in his plan for Salvation and the service of others.

Bro. Ricardo Grzona, frp
Fraternity of Ramón Pané

WHAT IS LECTIO DIVINA?

The illustration on the previous page depicts each of traditional step of *lectio divina* prayer, which is understood as the inspiration of the Holy Spirit that teaches us through the Scriptures to read, meditate, pray, contemplate, and act consistently. These are the five steps of *lectio divina*.

The clouds above the mountain represent the Holy Spirit, whom we call on to inspire us. This inspiration is represented by the rain. As this rain falls, it collects in a basin, forming a small alpine lake. This represents the first step of *lectio divina*: reading, in which we let the word of God deposit in us through the act of reading and rereading, filling the basin to form a lake. During this step, we ask the question, "What does the text say?"

Once the lake is full, it will overflow its basin. The water that escapes will then flow into a waterfall, which plunges downward, deeper. The action of the waterfall represents the second step of *lectio divina*: meditation. In this step, we deepen our understanding of the Scripture through meditation. We may ask the question, "What does the text say to me?"

As the waterfall continues, it will form a plunge pool. Here the water swirls around and mixes as it settles after falling. Due to the flow and agitation, it is a place with crystal-clear water, a place for cleansing. The recirculating and swirling pool represents the third step in *lectio divina*: prayer. During this step we give thanks or glory to God, ask for forgiveness, or simply converse with God. We ask questions such as, "How can I respond to your (God's) call?"

From the plunge pool, the flow of water enters a second descent in the form of rapids or a stepped waterfall. Here the water from on high descends to the valley, bringing the word of God down to the same plane on which we live. This is the fourth step of *lectio divina*: contemplation. In this step, we discern how to incorporate the word of God into our lives. As it descends to our level, our life, we may ask questions such as, "How do I reconcile my life with the word of God?"

As the rapids enter the valley, they slow and settle into a meandering river. This water gives us life, literally and spiritually. We use it for drinking, cultivation, and washing. Metaphorically, it represents the inspiration of the Holy Spirit, who descends from the clouds to the upper reaches of the mountain and down into the valley to where we live. The consistent flow and meandering of the river is the fifth and final step of *lectio divina*: action. In this step, we can draw from the water to act and live our lives according to the word of God, using the inspiration as a guide to help us discern our path in life.

1

YOU CALLED ME TO HAVE FAITH IN YOU

From Genesis 12

The Call of Abram

Now the LORD said to Abram, "Go from your country and your kindred and your father's house to the land that I will show you. I will make of you a great nation, and I will bless you, and make your name great, so that you will be a blessing. I will bless those who bless you, and the one who curses you I will curse; and in you all the families of the earth shall be blessed."

So Abram went, as the LORD had told him; and Lot went with him. Abram was seventy-five years old when he departed from Haran. Abram took his wife Sarai and his brother's son Lot, and all the possessions that they had gathered, and the persons whom they had acquired in Haran; and they set forth to go to the land of Canaan. When they had come to the land of Canaan, Abram passed through the land to the place at Shechem, to the oak of Moreh. At that time the Canaanites were in the land. Then the LORD appeared to Abram, and said, "To your offspring I will give this land." So he built there an altar to the LORD, who had appeared to him. From there he moved on to the hill country on the east of Bethel, and pitched his tent, with Bethel on the west and Ai on the east; and there he built an altar to the LORD and invoked the name of the LORD. And Abram journeyed on by stages toward the Negeb.

1 READING

After reading the passage once, read it a few more times.

Abram, who would later be renamed Abraham by God, is one of the first historical figures described in detail by the Bible. In this dialogue between Abraham and God, a story begins: our story, the story of God's plan for Salvation.

This passage opens with what is called *the theology of the promise*. In every call, God shows his desire for a radical change in the life of the person he calls, but he also promises signs of accompaniment. Note the promises and blessings in the verses: "I will make of you a great nation, and I will bless you, and make your name great, so that you will be a blessing." Notice that God takes the initiative in this conversation with Abraham. In order to follow God's call, Abraham would have had to accept God as the only true God, renounce all idols, and leave behind his home and many of his relatives. Yet God's promises were still very compelling. Abraham answers not with words but with action.

Who are the figures in these verses? How often do they appear?

Which action words in this passage are you most drawn to?

2 MEDITATION

Begin this step by considering the following ideas.

How do you feel that God calls you today? What does he call you to do?

What should your answer to God's call be?

Abraham had no children, yet God promised that he would have descendants. Do you think responding to God's call will be impossible?

How far will your faith take you? Is there a way you might measure your faith?

What is God asking you to leave behind?

What brings hope into your thoughts? Where does your hope lead your life?

Take a moment to examine your life. When the Lord offers you his promise of a new way of life, what are your doubts?

3 PRAYER

Respond to God in prayer, keeping in mind your reflections from the previous step.

Prayer is something spontaneous that comes from the heart. One way to pray is to reread the passage and recall what drew your attention the most. It is important to take this step in responding to the Lord before moving forward. Take your time; you can reread the text, reflect again on the questions in the meditation, and allow the prayer to flow.

Speak with the Lord about your concerns, your anxieties, your fears, and your limitations. Ask him to fill the empty places in your heart. Open yourself to God's suggestion so he can show you the path you must follow. "Go as he tells you," as Abraham did. You do not know what the road will be like, but you know the Lord. He will guide you.

4 CONTEMPLATION

Contemplate one idea from this reading for a while.

Reflect on the idea that God is communicating with you through this contemplation.

You may go back to some of the words and phrases from the Scripture, such as "leave," "I will make," and "I will bless."

Take hold of the idea that you will contemplate and sit with it for a while.

5 ACTION

Guided by God's word, resolve to begin a new life of faith.

Set a goal for yourself. The goal will be known only by you and the Lord. But it must be measurable, something you can accomplish. Take time to self-evaluate with this in mind. When you are ready, take the first steps toward this goal today.

2
YOU CALLED ME TO BE GRATEFUL

From Genesis 15

After these things the word of the LORD came to Abram in a vision, "Do not be afraid, Abram, I am your shield; your reward shall be very great." But Abram said, "O Lord GOD, what will you give me, for I continue childless, and the heir of my house is Eliezer of Damascus?" And Abram said, "You have given me no offspring, and so a slave born in my house is to be my heir." But the word of the LORD came to him, "This man shall not be your heir; no one but your very own issue shall be your heir." He brought him outside and said, "Look toward heaven and count the stars, if you are able to count them." Then he said to him, "So shall your descendants be." And he believed the LORD; and the LORD reckoned it to him as righteousness.

Then he said to him, "I am the LORD who brought you from Ur of the Chaldeans, to give you this land to possess." But he said, "O Lord GOD, how am I to know that I shall possess it?" He said to him, "Bring me a heifer three years old, a female goat three years old, a ram three years old, a turtledove, and a young pigeon." He brought him all these and cut them in two, laying each half over against the other; but he did not cut the birds in two. And when birds of prey came down on the carcasses, Abram drove them away.

As the sun was going down, a deep sleep fell upon Abram, and a deep and terrifying darkness descended upon him. Then the

LORD said to Abram, "Know this for certain, that your offspring shall be aliens in a land that is not theirs, and shall be slaves there, and they shall be oppressed for four hundred years; but I will bring judgment on the nation that they serve, and afterward they shall come out with great possessions. As for yourself, you shall go to your ancestors in peace; you shall be buried in a good old age. And they shall come back here in the fourth generation; for the iniquity of the Amorites is not yet complete."

When the sun had gone down and it was dark, a smoking fire pot and a flaming torch passed between these pieces. On that day the LORD made a covenant with Abram, saying, "To your descendants I give this land, from the river of Egypt to the great river, the river Euphrates."

1 READING

After reading the passage once, read it a few more times.

On your rereading, pay close attention to the action words in the text. Underline them, and return to these sections again. What do they say? Why does God insist so much on them?

2 MEDITATION

Begin this step by considering the following ideas.

Look at the sections you underlined. Identify your fears in order to begin a spiritual journey. What are you afraid of? Put your fears at the feet of the Lord and acknowledge them.

When is it hard for you to trust the Lord? Identify areas in which you could trust more in him, and ask the Lord to help you trust his infinite wisdom. Remember: He will never disappoint you.

3 PRAYER

Respond to God in prayer, keeping in mind your reflections from the previous step.

Do the same exercise God asked of Abraham: Step outside on a starry night to look at the stars and try to count them. How many are out there? Let your sense of wonder be your prayer. Give thanks for everything God provides for you.

4 CONTEMPLATION

Contemplate one idea from this reading for a while.

Do not be afraid.

Ponder the stars.

5 ACTION

Guided by God's word, resolve to begin a new life of faith.

What will this new way of life be like? Will it align with God's plan? Make it real. Act on it.

3
YOU CALLED ME TO TRUST IN YOU

From Genesis 22

After these things God tested Abraham. He said to him, "Abraham!" And he said, "Here I am." He said, "Take your son, your only son Isaac, whom you love, and go to the land of Moriah, and offer him there as a burnt offering on one of the mountains that I shall show you." So Abraham rose early in the morning, saddled his donkey, and took two of his young men with him, and his son Isaac; he cut the wood for the burnt offering, and set out and went to the place in the distance that God had shown him. On the third day Abraham looked up and saw the place far away. Then Abraham said to his young men, "Stay here with the donkey; the boy and I will go over there; we will worship, and then we will come back to you." Abraham took the wood of the burnt offering and laid it on his son Isaac, and he himself carried the fire and the knife. So the two of them walked on together. Isaac said to his father Abraham, "Father!" And he said, "Here I am, my son." He said, "The fire and the wood are here, but where is the lamb for a burnt offering?" Abraham said, "God himself will provide the lamb for a burnt offering, my son." So the two of them walked on together.

When they came to the place that God had shown him, Abraham built an altar there and laid the wood in order. He bound his son Isaac, and laid him on the altar, on top of the wood. Then Abraham reached out his hand and took the knife to kill his son. But the angel of the LORD called to him from heaven, and said, "Abraham, Abraham!" And he said, "Here I am." He said, "Do not lay your hand on the boy or do anything to him; for now I know that you fear God, since you have not withheld your son, your only son, from me." And Abraham looked up and saw a ram, caught in a thicket by its horns. Abraham went and took the ram and offered it up as a burnt offering instead of his son. So Abraham called that place "The LORD will provide"; as it is said to this day, "On the mount of the LORD it shall be provided."

The angel of the LORD called to Abraham a second time from heaven, and said, "By myself I have sworn, says the LORD: Because you have done this, and have not withheld your son, your only son, I will indeed bless you, and I will make your offspring as numerous as the stars of heaven and as the sand that is on the seashore. And your offspring shall possess the gate of their enemies, and by your offspring shall all the nations of the earth gain blessing for themselves, because you have obeyed my voice."

1 READING

After reading the passage once, read it a few more times.

Here we find an especially difficult situation. Abraham receives a strange message: He must sacrifice his son, Isaac, to God. Abraham obeys, but God stops him just as he is going to kill his own son. Eventually, Isaac will come to represent the people of Israel, and even in the most difficult of times, God will deliver them from evil.

This reading also gives a sense of being rewarded for obedience. To listen to the voice of God is to obey, even when we don't understand his commands. To listen is to be attentive, and most of all, to be available; God blesses those who listen and obey.

2 MEDITATION

Begin this step by considering the following ideas.

Have you ever been in a difficult situation when you felt you did not have a choice? What was your first reaction?

Do you realize that although the roads God offers are at times difficult, or seemingly meaningless, he always has a plan?

How is the situation of Abraham and Isaac similar to yours?

3 PRAYER

Respond to God in prayer, keeping in mind your reflections from the previous step.

Think of the most difficult moments you remember in your own life. Present them to the Lord as your own sacrifice. Offer God your sorrows in prayer. These are the things you do not understand about your life. He will receive them and return them to you transformed.

Be obedient, like Abraham. You do not know what the road ahead will be, or what trials you will have to face. But you can trust that the Lord will guide you.

4 CONTEMPLATION

Contemplate one idea from this reading for a while.

Take the idea you choose to focus on, and think about the blessings you receive from God. Know that God is communicating with you through that idea. Perhaps it is a call to return to God's promise: "I will bless you."

5 ACTION

Guided by God's word, resolve to begin a new life of faith.

What will your life be like as you become aware of the blessings that God grants you? What will it mean to live with faith?

Set a personal goal. This goal will be known only by you and the Lord, but it must be measurable and attainable.

4

YOU CALLED ME TO BEGIN A JOURNEY

From Genesis 28

Jacob left Beer-sheba and went toward Haran. He came to a certain place and stayed there for the night, because the sun had set. Taking one of the stones of the place, he put it under his head and lay down in that place. And he dreamed that there was a ladder set up on the earth, the top of it reaching to heaven; and the angels of God were ascending and descending on it. And the LORD stood beside him and said, "I am the Lord, the God of Abraham your father and the God of Isaac; the land on which you lie I will give to you and to your offspring; and your offspring shall be like the dust of the earth, and you shall spread abroad to the west and to the east and to the north and to the south; and all the families of the earth shall be blessed in you and in your offspring. Know that I am with you and will keep you wherever you go, and will bring you back to this land; for I will not leave you until I have done what I have promised you." Then Jacob woke from his sleep and said, "Surely the LORD is in this place—and I did not know it!" And he was afraid, and said, "How awesome is this place! This is none other than the house of God, and this is the gate of heaven."

So Jacob rose early in the morning, and he took the stone that he had put under his head and set it up for a pillar and poured oil on the top of it. He called that place Bethel; but the name of the city was Luz at the first. Then Jacob made a vow, saying,

"If God will be with me, and will keep me in this way that I go, and will give me bread to eat and clothing to wear, so that I come again to my father's house in peace, then the LORD shall be my God, and this stone, which I have set up for a pillar, shall be God's house; and of all that you give me I will surely give one-tenth to you."

1 READING

After reading the passage once, read it a few more times.

In the Scriptures, we find that God often communicates through dreams. In this case, it is Jacob who has a dream. He dreams of a ladder that rests on the earth and reaches to heaven. The fathers of the Church used this text when they defined the *lectio divina* exercises as a ladder leading to God and heaven. The steps of this prayer remind us of that ladder.

The important thing to remember from this reading is that from this moment on, Jacob, who is later called Israel, asks God for his company and to keep him safe.

2 MEDITATION

Begin this step by considering the following ideas.

God calls us in many ways. How do you figure out that God is communicating with you and calling you?

Are you attentive to the ways in which God does this?

God also speaks to you through the actions of others and promises to stay close to you. Are you aware of this?

Do you ask God to stay close to you and take care of you?

3 PRAYER

Respond to God in prayer, keeping in mind your reflections from the previous step.

Praying with God's word can also lead us to reread the same text in the form of prayer and to make Jacob's prayer our own. For your prayer, find an excerpt from the reading, or use this one: "Stay with me and accompany me on the journey of my life."

4 CONTEMPLATION

Contemplate one idea from this reading for a while.

Come, stay with me, and protect me always, Lord.

Show me the way to you.

The Lord shall be my God.

5 ACTION

Guided by God's word, resolve to begin a new life of faith.

In the journey with God, you must decide to choose the path he shows you. Commit to receive his blessings and take strength every day from the Lord by reading his word and through daily prayer. This practice will guide you on the path to him.

5
YOU CALLED ME TO DREAM BIG

From Genesis 41

Joseph answered Pharaoh, "It is not I; God will give Pharaoh a favorable answer." Then Pharaoh said to Joseph, "In my dream I was standing on the banks of the Nile; and seven cows, fat and sleek, came up out of the Nile and fed in the reed grass. Then seven other cows came up after them, poor, very ugly, and thin. Never had I seen such ugly ones in all the land of Egypt. The thin and ugly cows ate up the first seven fat cows, but when they had eaten them no one would have known that they had done so, for they were still as ugly as before. Then I awoke. I fell asleep a second time and I saw in my dream seven ears of grain, full and good, growing on one stalk, and seven ears, withered, thin, and blighted by the east wind, sprouting after them; and the thin ears swallowed up the seven good ears. But when I told it to the magicians, there was no one who could explain it to me."

Then Joseph said to Pharaoh, "Pharaoh's dreams are one and the same; God has revealed to Pharaoh what he is about to do. The seven good cows are seven years, and the seven good ears are seven years; the dreams are one. The seven lean and ugly cows that came up after them are seven years, as are the seven empty ears blighted by the east wind. They are seven years of famine. It is as I told Pharaoh; God has shown to Pharaoh what he is about to do. There will come seven years of great plenty throughout all the land of Egypt. After them there will arise seven years of famine, and all the plenty will be forgotten in the land of Egypt; the famine will consume the land. The plenty will no longer be known in the land because of the famine that will follow, for it will be very grievous. And the doubling of Pharaoh's dream means that the thing is fixed by God, and God will shortly bring it about. Now therefore let Pharaoh select a man who is discerning and wise, and set him over the land of Egypt. Let Pharaoh proceed to appoint overseers over the land, and take one-fifth of the produce of the land of Egypt during the seven plenteous years. Let them gather all the food of these good years that are coming, and lay up grain under the authority of Pharaoh for food in the cities, and let them keep it. That food shall be a reserve for the land against the seven years of famine that are to befall the land of Egypt, so that the land may not perish through the famine."

1 READING

After reading the passage once, read it a few more times.

We are again faced with a dream that must be interpreted. We know Joseph was an expert in this skill from previous stories in the Scriptures. His brothers did not like him because he had won the love of his father, Israel. That is why they sold him as a slave, and he ended up in a prison in Egypt.

Pharaoh had dreams that no one could interpret. Joseph's former cellmate remembered that Joseph knew how to interpret dreams. So they brought Joseph to interpret Pharaoh's dream. He did so with such skill and gave such wise advice to Pharaoh, that Pharaoh appointed him viceroy of Egypt.

An important point from this reading is to notice how God, even in the most difficult situations, prepares people to carry out his plan for our Salvation, which has been written with many sacrifices and hardships, like those Joseph experienced.

2 MEDITATION

Begin this step by considering the following ideas.

God continues to call his people. As God's chosen, we must go through trials that at first sight seem insurmountable.

What trials have you gone through that you have not considered part of God's plan? Can you interpret these as part of it?

Is your vision like Joseph's? Are you always willing to interpret what God shows you in his own way as part of his plan for you?

3 PRAYER

Respond to God in prayer, keeping in mind your reflections from the previous step.

Praying with God's word leads us to be like Joseph, unafraid of our dreams.

Today in your prayer, ask God to let you dream.

Dream God's dreams, where you are willingly contributing to God's plan in a significant way.

Ask God for the ability to see yourself in your dreams as part of his plan, as he envisions you contributing to it.

4 CONTEMPLATION

Contemplate one idea from this reading for a while.

"Select a man (or woman) who is discerning and wise, and set him (or her) over the land."

Visualize a dream the Lord wants you to have and how you would fulfill the role that he has planned for you.

5 ACTION

Guided by God's word, resolve to begin a new life of faith.

When we allow ourselves to dream through God's word, we practice finding ways to change our lives according to his plan.

6

YOU CALLED ME TO BE AN AGENT OF CHANGE

From Exodus 3

Moses was keeping the flock of his father-in-law Jethro, the priest of Midian; he led his flock beyond the wilderness, and came to Horeb, the mountain of God. There the angel of the LORD appeared to him in a flame of fire out of a bush; he looked, and the bush was blazing, yet it was not consumed. Then Moses said, "I must turn aside and look at this great sight, and see why the bush is not burned up." When the LORD saw that he had turned aside to see, God called to him out of the bush, "Moses, Moses!" And he said, "Here I am." Then he said, "Come no closer! Remove the sandals from your feet, for the place on which you are standing is holy ground." He said further, "I am the God of your father, the God of Abraham, the God of Isaac, and the God of Jacob." And Moses hid his face, for he was afraid to look at God.

Then the LORD said, "I have observed the misery of my people who are in Egypt; I have heard their cry on account of their taskmasters. Indeed, I know their sufferings, and I have come down to deliver them from the Egyptians, and to bring them up out of that land to a good and broad land, a land flowing with milk and honey, to the country of the Canaanites, the Hittites, the Amorites, the Perizzites, the Hivites, and the Jebusites."

1 READING

After reading the passage once, read it a few more times.

Moses had fled from Egypt. He was afraid. He preferred his comfortable and anonymous life in the desert, where he got married and cared for his father-in-law's flock. But God, who sees everything and calls his people to their purpose, sought Moses out in the desert.

He chose a special way to do this: through a natural phenomenon, the burning bush. Then he asked Moses to take off his sandals, to enter barefoot in the presence of the Lord, showing respect for the holy ground he was standing on.

God also showed that he hears the prayers and needs of his people. God acts through intermediaries, by calling his messengers and others to carry out his plan through his inspiration.

It didn't matter that Moses was afraid, that he stuttered, or that he had other impairments. God had chosen him and would give him all the necessary means to free his people from slavery.

Moses, despite the odds of losing to the great Pharaoh, would be the great liberator of his people because God had chosen him. He will forever be remembered as one who answered God's call and overcame great odds with the help of the Lord, despite his own limitations.

2 MEDITATION

Begin this step by considering the following ideas.

When God calls us, we may see ourselves, with our human imperfections, as not meeting his requirements. In our own eyes, we don't measure up to the tasks he intends for us.

When you look at yourself, do you think that because you don't see how you meet all the requirements of God's great plans, your calling should be limited to being a "good Christian"?

Maybe you, like Moses, have hidden in the shadows and remained anonymous in a Christian life that is simple and hassle-free. But God is calling you to a greater existence.

There are many people around you who are in need. Could the Lord be asking you to take some action on their behalf?

Do you feel that you have a clear and defined mission to carry out in the name of God? What could that mission be?

The person who approaches the Scriptures prayerfully will find this calling as the reason for a new way of life.

When you realize that God sees you, you might feel ashamed of all your flaws. But God looks to you anyway, and he wants to make you a part of his plan for the salvation of all humanity.

Do not deny this opportunity. Come out from your hiding place in the desert, and step into the light of God's inspiration. The words you speak will not be your own—they will be the Lord's. Do not be afraid.

3 PRAYER

Respond to God in prayer, keeping in mind your reflections from the previous step.

Praying with God's word leads us to new attitudes.

It is true that we might feel shame at being seen by God, but he doesn't call us in order to make us feel bad. He calls us in order to ask for our cooperation.

As an act of humility, let us recognize that the Lord of life wants us to help carry out his plan by saving others. We are part of his plan of salvation. Put yourself in the presence of the Lord. Take off your sandals; that is, set aside anything that distracts you or makes noise.

Read the Bible passage once again. Give thanks to God for choosing you, and ask him to illuminate your path, your journey, and your unique contributions to the Church and his plan for Salvation.

Make this a moment of calm, without rush, and without fear.

4 CONTEMPLATION

Contemplate one idea from this reading for a while.

"I have seen the oppression of my people."

"I send you to free the oppressed."

"I want you to be my messenger."

"You will speak in my Name."

5 ACTION

Guided by God's word, resolve to begin a new life of faith.

In life, there are moments when you must make big decisions. Upon reading this text of Moses' call, pursue a significant change in yourself. What will you do to leave the anonymous life of a comfortable Christianity? How will you prove that you are indeed a unique actor in God's plan for Salvation?

7

YOU CALLED ME TO BE A
LEADER TO MY PEOPLE

From Joshua 1

After the death of Moses the servant of the LORD, the LORD spoke to Joshua son of Nun, Moses' assistant, saying, "My servant Moses is dead. Now proceed to cross the Jordan, you and all this people, into the land that I am giving to them, to the Israelites. Every place that the sole of your foot will tread upon I have given to you, as I promised to Moses. From the wilderness and the Lebanon as far as the great river, the river Euphrates, all the land of the Hittites, to the Great Sea in the west shall be your territory. No one shall be able to stand against you all the days of your life. As I was with Moses, so I will be with you; I will not fail you or forsake you. Be strong and courageous; for you shall put this people in possession of the land that I swore to their ancestors to give them. Only be strong and very courageous, being careful to act in accordance with all the law that my servant Moses commanded you; do not turn from it to the right hand or to the left, so that you may be successful wherever you go. This book of the law shall not depart out of your mouth; you shall meditate on it day and night, so that you may be careful to act in accordance with all that is written in it. For then you shall make your way prosperous, and then you shall be successful. I hereby command you: Be strong and courageous; do not be frightened or dismayed, for the LORD your God is with you wherever you go."

1 READING

After reading the passage once, read it a few more times.

Moses led the Israelites out of Egypt. However, because he doubted, God assured him that he would never enter the Promised Land. God allowed Moses only to see the Promised Land from a distant mountain, and then Moses died.

God chose Joshua as Moses' successor. God prepared him for that role, but Joshua was afraid. For this reason, God reminded him that he would not abandon him. "Be strong and courageous," God said. But above all things, he asked Joshua to always remind the people of God's word, to never deviate from the Law. God assured him that if he put this into practice, he would succeed.

2 MEDITATION

Begin this step by considering the following ideas.

Do you truly believe that the Lord calls you to carry out his plan?

What can you do to tune into God's call?

Are you committed to respond to his call?

Are you afraid to act according to the Lord's request? Can you name these fears that keep you from actively contributing to God's plan?

Do you hear the Lord encouraging you to be strong and courageous in your faith?

3 PRAYER

Respond to God in prayer, keeping in mind your reflections from the previous step.

Thank you, Lord, for your saving word, your love, and your mercy.

Thank you for changing the perception I have often had of you. You are never far, and you call me to follow you, to be your disciple, and to be an actor in your plan for salvation.

Give me the grace to be willing to listen to your call. I want to imitate you, to go out and seek those who are lost or forgotten. Give me a courageous heart to reach out to all who are in need in your name and with your mercy.

4 CONTEMPLATION

Contemplate one idea from this reading for a while.

"I hereby command you: Be strong and courageous; do not be frightened or dismayed, for the LORD your God is with you wherever you go."

With this in mind, enter contemplation, asking the Lord to help you be courageous.

5 ACTION

Guided by God's word, resolve to begin a new life of faith.

This is a good time to make an examination of conscience and remember the many times the Lord has passed through your life without you noticing him. Recognize and acknowledge these moments. You might ask for forgiveness and decide to let go of your fears. If it feels right, you might start a conversation with a friend about your encounters with God.

8

YOU CALLED ME TO BE AT THE SERVICE OF YOUR HOUSE

From the First Book of Samuel 3

Now the boy Samuel was ministering to the LORD under Eli. The word of the LORD was rare in those days; visions were not widespread.

At that time Eli, whose eyesight had begun to grow dim so that he could not see, was lying down in his room; the lamp of God had not yet gone out, and Samuel was lying down in the temple of the LORD, where the ark of God was. Then the LORD called, "Samuel! Samuel!" and he said, "Here I am!" and ran to Eli, and said, "Here I am, for you called me." But he said, "I did not call; lie down again." So he went and lay down. The LORD called again, "Samuel!" Samuel got up and went to Eli, and said, "Here I am, for you called me." But he said, "I did not call, my son; lie down again." Now Samuel did not yet know the LORD, and the word of the LORD had not yet been revealed to him. The LORD called Samuel again, a third time. And he got up and went to Eli, and said, "Here I am, for you called me." Then Eli perceived that the LORD was calling the boy. Therefore Eli said to Samuel, "Go, lie down; and if he calls you, you shall say, 'Speak, LORD, for your servant is listening.'" So Samuel went and lay down in his place.

Now the LORD came and stood there, calling as before, "Samuel! Samuel!" And Samuel said, "Speak, for your servant is listening."

1 READING

After reading the passage once, read it a few more times.

When God calls us, he does not see us in the same way that we, as human beings, see ourselves. He wants to entrust us with a mission. In Samuel's case, even though he was very young, God chose him for a reason, a mission.

It can be difficult to hear God calling us in the midst of so many other voices. We get confused by all the chatter around us.

For this reason, it is very important to be attentive and to have a good guide. In spiritual life, we cannot proceed alone—to do so would be arrogant. In this scripture passage, Eli helps Samuel understand that God is calling him.

2 MEDITATION

Begin this step by considering the following ideas.

God calls us continuously. Here, we see Samuel, still a child but nevertheless called by God. Do you feel you are too young to be involved in the matters of God?

This reading is a reminder that there are no excuses in responding to God. Not our age nor our training nor our shortcomings serve as an excuse.

Being a Christian is more than participating in rites, traditions, and celebrations. Being a Christian means living a virtuous life of constant listening.

Remember: Listening is a way of accepting.

3 PRAYER

Respond to God in prayer, keeping in mind your reflections from the previous step.

Praying with God's word is an invitation to be attentive and to listen without fear. Sometimes we get confused by the many voices we hear. People may pretend to speak in God's name, but we must tune into the true word of God in Scripture.

Prayerfully reread the text several times. Approach it with a listening attitude that is, an attitude of acceptance. Take the time you need to listen to God. If possible, try to be in a place with minimal distractions while you do this.

Ask the Lord to show you how to listen to him and accept him.

4 CONTEMPLATION

Contemplate one idea from this reading for a while.

"Speak Lord, for your servant listens."

"Speak Lord, for your servant accepts."

5 ACTION

Guided by God's word, resolve to begin a new life of faith.

Return to the "listening attitude," so that the Lord may speak to you. Is God asking you to speak in his name, what will you say?

9

YOU CALLED ME TO SEE THE GREATNESS IN OTHERS

From the First Book of Samuel 16

When they came, he looked on Eli'ab and thought, "Surely the Lord's anointed is before him." But the LORD said to Samuel, "Do not look on his appearance or on the height of his stature, because I have rejected him; for the LORD sees not as man sees; man looks on the outward appearance, but the LORD looks on the heart." Then Jesse called Abin'adab, and made him pass before Samuel. And he said, "Neither has the Lord chosen this one." Then Jesse made Shammah pass by. And he said, "Neither has the LORD chosen this one." And Jesse made seven of his sons pass before Samuel. And Samuel said to Jesse, "The LORD has not chosen these." And Samuel said to Jesse, "Are all your sons here?" And he said, "There remains yet the youngest, but behold, he is keeping the sheep." And Samuel said to Jesse, "Send and fetch him; for we will not sit down till he comes here." And he sent, and brought him in. Now he was ruddy, and had beautiful eyes, and was handsome. And the LORD said, "Arise, anoint him; for this is he." Then Samuel took the horn of oil, and anointed him in the midst of his brothers; and the Spirit of the LORD came mightily upon David from that day forward. And Samuel rose up, and went to Ramah.

1 READING

After reading the passage once, read it a few more times.

The prophet Samuel realized that King Saul was not a very religious man and had drifted far from God's plan. Therefore, Samuel felt disappointed, and God, who always listens to the cries of his people, sent him to anoint a new king.

God gave him a clear message:

> "Do not look on his appearance or on the height of his stature, because I have rejected him; for the LORD sees not as man sees; man looks on the outward appearance, but the LORD looks on the heart."

All of Jesse's sons came to Samuel, but the king chosen by God was not among them. But Jesse had another son, the youngest one, the one no human would have chosen, the one who tended the flock in the field: David.

God chooses according to the heart, not by outward appearance or worldly status.

2 MEDITATION

Begin this step by considering the following ideas.

How often do you complain to God about things not being the way you would like?

Humans discriminate when they fail to see as God does, when they fail to see the heart of the person. Discrimination is a serious sin, and unfortunately, it is quite common.

Have you ever felt discriminated against? Has this experience contributed to an attitude that might lead you to do the same? How can this cycle be broken?

When God chooses, he does not judge by outward appearance, he sees the heart of the person. Do you fear God seeing you?

Some people feel small and unprepared for the mission God has intended for them. Do you feel this way? To what extent do the limitations you put on yourself prevent you from responding to God?

Remember: God does not choose us according to our qualifications, but he equips us with what we need to carry out our part of his plan.

3 PRAYER

Respond to God in prayer, keeping in mind your reflections from the previous step.

Lord, I want to stand in your presence with what I have, as I am. I place into your hands my virtues and my imperfections. I do not want to withhold anything from you.

I believe I am chosen by you. I feel what David felt as a humble shepherd, whom you chose to be the shepherd of your people.

Encountering you changes me and renews me. It gives me a different perspective with which to face my new life with you. Give me the light I need to be able to see what you ask of me and increase my will to make good decisions and carry them out.

Amen.

4 CONTEMPLATION

Contemplate one idea from this reading for a while.

> "The LORD sees not as man sees; man looks on the outward appearance, but the Lord looks on the heart."

5 ACTION

Guided by God's word, resolve to begin a new life of faith.

Decide on a specific action you can take to respond to God's call. Show through your actions that you are convinced that the Lord calls you, and you are committed to responding to him. Resolve to live honestly the vocation to which you are being called. Share the joy you feel from making this commitment with others.

10
YOU CALLED ME TO BE ACTIVE

From Isaiah 6

In the year that King Uzziah died, I saw the Lord sitting on a throne, high and lofty; and the hem of his robe filled the temple. Seraphs were in attendance above him; each had six wings: with two they covered their faces, and with two they covered their feet, and with two they flew. And one called to another and said:

"Holy, holy, holy is the LORD of hosts;
the whole earth is full of his glory."

The pivots on the thresholds shook at the voices of those who called, and the house filled with smoke. And I said: "Woe is me! I am lost, for I am a man of unclean lips, and I live among a people of unclean lips; yet my eyes have seen the King, the LORD of hosts!"

Then one of the seraphs flew to me, holding a live coal that had been taken from the altar with a pair of tongs. The seraph touched my mouth with it and said: "Now that this has touched your lips, your guilt has departed and your sin is blotted out." Then I heard the voice of the Lord saying, "Whom shall I send, and who will go for us?" And I said, "Here am I; send me!"

1 READING

After reading the passage once, read it a few more times.

The prophets didn't always know right away that God was calling them. However, we can see that there is a moment when the person being called realizes that God needs him or her to take immediate action. This knowing may have come as a vision, a feeling, or a clear realization.

This passage begins mentioning the death of King Uzziah. The whole passage is full of signs that highlight the divine nature of the prophet's vision and its impact on him.

Isaiah presents himself to the Lord, God, and with great resolve and generosity states his willingness to accept his commission.

2 MEDITATION

Begin this step by considering the following ideas.

In the face of concrete needs, God calls people to respond with solutions in his name.

Isaiah's calling reminds us that there are many needs for which God calls us specifically.

More than letting ourselves be carried away by all the signs of God's presence, we must understand the most basic request, when God says, "Whom shall I send, and who will go for us?"

Have you considered that the Lord still needs to send someone on his behalf to proclaim his word to others?

How do you react to God's call? Are you available? Will you respond, like Isaiah, "Here am I; send me!"?

Are you starting to understand where the Lord is sending you? Maybe it is not a place but a direction: toward the fringes of society, to those who need to hear the good news of God's word.

Do not be afraid if you do not understand the path you must take. The important thing now is to accept the Lord's call.

Remember: God does not choose the ones who are qualified; he equips those he chooses with what they will need.

3 PRAYER

Respond to God in prayer, keeping in mind your reflections from the previous step.

Lord, today I can see many needs among your people, especially in those who have not yet come to know the good news of your word.

Lord, fear sometimes paralyzes me. And it is because of the fear that I will disappoint others that I make the wrong choices.

I want to be at your disposal. You know that I am not perfect and that I have many shortcomings, but I know you need me to be your messenger. Even though I do not fully understand how I will respond, today I accept your call.

My prayer is the same as Isaiah's: "Here am I; send me!" Amen.

4 CONTEMPLATION

Contemplate one idea from this reading for a while.

"Here am I; send me!"

5 ACTION

Guided by God's word, resolve to begin a new life of faith.

How can you bring the word of the Lord to those who have not yet heard it or who have distanced themselves from their faith? What actions can you take to demonstrate to others the joy and goodness that come from faith in God?

It may be a long process for others to recognize how the word of God enlightens your life. Are you committed to living out your calling?

11

YOU CALLED ME TO BELIEVE IN MYSELF

From Jeremiah 1

Now the word of the LORD came to me saying,

"Before I formed you in the womb I knew you,
   and before you were born I consecrated you;
   I appointed you a prophet to the nations."

Then I said, "Ah, LORD GOD! Truly I do not know how to speak, for I am only a boy." But the LORD said to me,

"Do not say, "I am only a boy";
for you shall go to all to whom I send you,
and you shall speak whatever I command you.
Do not be afraid of them,
for I am with you to deliver you,
   says the LORD."

Then the LORD put out his hand and touched my mouth; and the LORD said to me,

"Now I have put my words in your mouth.
See, today I appoint you over nations and over kingdoms,
to pluck up and to pull down,
to destroy and to overthrow,
to build and to plant."

The word of the LORD came to me, saying, "Jeremiah, what do you see?" And I said, "I see a branch of an almond tree." Then the LORD said to me, "You have seen well, for I am watching over my word to perform it."

1 READING

After reading the passage once, read it a few more times.

The prophet Jeremiah realizes that God is the "Eternal One." God was alive before him, and in this eternity, he has chosen Jeremiah as a prophet for all nations. God is outside of time, and he is also "owner" of all things, including time. He decides, he chooses, and he calls.

Typically, when we are called by God, we make many excuses. Here, Jeremiah says that he is still too young. But God demands that Jeremiah go wherever God sends him and say what God asks him to say. God directly commands Jeremiah to do this.

God puts his words into the prophet's mouth. Whatever Jeremiah speaks will be inspired by the word of God and will not be in his own words. And God's word is always fulfilled.

2 MEDITATION

Begin this step by considering the following ideas.

God chose you to be exactly who you are and not someone else. Remember that you are the one who was chosen by God for the life you have. Your life is part of his plan. What is your first reaction when you think of your life in this way, as a gift from God?

Many people complain about their lives, perhaps because they feel pressure to meet standards imposed on them by society or because they have trouble keeping up with trends they see. However, life itself is something to be grateful for every day.

Jeremiah made excuses to avoid his mission. What excuses do you make to avoid your calling? Make a mental list of the excuses you use frequently and offer it to the Lord. What does he tell you about your excuses?

Now turn your attention to your daily life. Do you dedicate time to prayer and reading God's word? Do you know that this is a way to allow the Lord to speak through you?

Conclude by looking around you. Reflect on your community, the places you frequent, and the places you do not go—are there places you avoid? Where do you feel that the Lord is sending you?

3 PRAYER

Respond to God in prayer, keeping in mind your reflections from the previous step.

Thank you, Lord, because before you created the world and all that exists, in your eternity, you had already chosen me to live. Thank you, Lord, for the life you give me.

Even with the struggles I face, my life is totally different from that of others. You have given me a unique and special mission, entrusted only to me. And only through my life, with the gifts you have given me, will it be possible to fulfill this mission.

I pray that you grant me inner strength to align my will with your plan. Let me go, Lord, out into the world, proclaiming your word, holding steadfast to it.

Amen.

4 CONTEMPLATION

Contemplate one idea from this reading for a while.

> "Before I formed you in the womb I knew you,
> and before you were born I consecrated you;
> I appointed you a prophet to the nations."

5 ACTION

Guided by God's word, resolve to begin a new life of faith.

To be a prophet is to proclaim the kingdom of God and to denounce everything that opposes it. What a prophet says is not always welcomed. If you speak in God's name, you should know that many who hear you will not receive the message well, because it may disrupt their perception of the world.

> "Do not be afraid of them,
> for I am with you to deliver you."

What value from God's word will you proclaim?

12

YOU CALLED ME TO SPEAK UP

Ezekiel 3

He said to me, O mortal, eat what is offered to you; eat this scroll, and go, speak to the house of Israel. So I opened my mouth, and he gave me the scroll to eat. He said to me, Mortal, eat this scroll that I give you and fill your stomach with it. Then I ate it; and in my mouth it was as sweet as honey.

He said to me: Mortal, go to the house of Israel and speak my very words to them. For you are not sent to a people of obscure speech and difficult language, but to the house of Israel—not to many peoples of obscure speech and difficult language, whose words you cannot understand. Surely, if I sent you to them, they would listen to you. But the house of Israel will not listen to you, for they are not willing to listen to me; because all the house of Israel have a hard forehead and a stubborn heart. See, I have made your face hard against their faces, and your forehead hard against their foreheads. Like the hardest stone, harder than flint, I have made your forehead; do not fear them or be dismayed at their looks, for they are a rebellious house. He said to me: Mortal, all my words that I shall speak to you receive in your heart and hear with your ears; then go to the exiles, to your people, and speak to them. Say to them, "Thus says the Lord GOD"; whether they hear or refuse to hear.

Then the spirit lifted me up, and as the glory of the Lord rose from its place, I heard behind me the sound of loud rumbling; it was the sound of the wings of the living creatures brushing against one another, and the sound of the wheels beside them, that sounded like a loud rumbling. The spirit lifted me up and bore me away; I went in bitterness in the heat of my spirit, the hand of the Lord being strong upon me.

1 READING

After reading the passage once, read it a few more times.

The reading of Ezekiel's calling begins with a metaphor: He must eat the scroll of the word; that is, he must introduce God's word into his life. And he explains that the word was sweet as honey. But immediately after it is consumed, God's word must be transmitted. God makes clear to him: "Speak my very words to them."

Listen carefully to all of God's word and take it into your heart. Then share it, even if others do not listen. You must proclaim his word.

God says once again, "Do not fear." These are words that God repeats in every call he makes to entrust his people with a mission. Overcome your fear. The Lord gives strength to those he calls.

2 MEDITATION

Begin this step by considering the following ideas.

How often do you enjoy reading or hearing God's word? Do you read the Bible prayerfully and in depth? Do you find it to be "sweet as honey" and nourishment for life, as Ezekiel did?

Do you know in your heart that receiving God's word is not to acquire knowledge about the Bible but to lead a new life, a new life in which the Lord nourishes us to fulfill his plan that we live as Jesus did?

What are the obstacles you face in proclaiming the Gospel, particularly to people who are stubborn in their rejection of the word?

Do you know in your heart that as Christians our mission is to return what was given to us?

Let us also look at the state of our world, where there are still many people who have not received the gift of faith in God. Considering this, what choice do you have?

3 PRAYER

Respond to God in prayer, keeping in mind your reflections from the previous step.

Holy Father, I thank you because you chose me to be nourished by your word. I am aware that many people still do not know you, or if they do, for some reason they have wandered.

I understand that you are calling me to give a specific response, to spread your word.

I confess, Lord, that I am afraid. Even with everything you have given me and the nourishment you have provided, fear persists. Give me the courage to proclaim you to those who still do not know you.

I want to be your prophet, Lord; thank you for choosing me and for accepting me as I am. I am here to do your will.

Amen.

4 CONTEMPLATION

Contemplate one idea from this reading for a while.

> "Eat this scroll, and go, speak to the house of Israel."

5 ACTION

Guided by God's word, resolve to begin a new life of faith.

To whom will you proclaim the good news? Will it be anyone in particular or everyone you encounter?

13

YOU CALLED ME TO LIFE

Psalm 139

O LORD, you have searched me and known me.
You know when I sit down and when I rise up;
  you discern my thoughts from far away.
You search out my path and my lying down,
  and are acquainted with all my ways.
Even before a word is on my tongue,
  O LORD, you know it completely.
You hem me in, behind and before,
  and lay your hand upon me.
Such knowledge is too wonderful for me;
  it is so high that I cannot attain it.

Where can I go from your spirit?
  Or where can I flee from your presence?
If I ascend to heaven, you are there;
  if I make my bed in Sheol, you are there.
If I take the wings of the morning
  and settle at the farthest limits of the sea,
even there your hand shall lead me,
  and your right hand shall hold me fast.
If I say, "Surely the darkness shall cover me,
  and the light around me become night,"
even the darkness is not dark to you;
  the night is as bright as the day,

for darkness is as light to you.
For it was you who formed my inward parts;
    you knit me together in my mother's womb.
I praise you, for I am fearfully and wonderfully made.
    Wonderful are your works;
that I know very well.
    My frame was not hidden from you,
when I was being made in secret,
    intricately woven in the depths of the earth.
Your eyes beheld my unformed substance.
In your book were written
    all the days that were formed for me,
    when none of them as yet existed.
How weighty to me are your thoughts, O God!
    How vast is the sum of them!
I try to count them—they are more than the sand;
    I come to the end—I am still with you.

O that you would kill the wicked, O God,
    and that the bloodthirsty would depart from me—
those who speak of you maliciously,
    and lift themselves up against you for evil!
Do I not hate those who hate you, O Lord?
    And do I not loathe those who rise up against you?
I hate them with perfect hatred;
    I count them my enemies.
Search me, O God, and know my heart;
    test me and know my thoughts.
See if there is any wicked way in me,
    and lead me in the way everlasting.

1 READING

After reading the passage once, read it a few more times.

The Lord, from the beginning, is the one who knows you and searches your thoughts. Let him call you through your reading.

Use a highlighter or a pen to mark those sentences that most catch your attention. These might be the lines you identify with, those that raise questions about your life, or those in which you feel God is speaking to you directly.

2 MEDITATION

Begin this step by considering the following ideas.

God has kept watch over you, at every step, from the way your father's and mother's seed joined in the womb to the way you formed and grew. Imagine all this. God oversaw this!

Why? From among millions of sperm, God allowed the one that formed you, not another, to fertilize your mother's egg—he chose that one specifically to form you. You are unique. You are unlike anyone else. You have never existed before, and there will never be anyone like you again.

When have you felt that God did not see you? Have you ever felt that you could do whatever you wanted?

What part of your life do you think the Lord is examining closely? What changes can you make in your life to live more closely in response to his call?

What does Psalm 139 say to you? What does it ask of you?

3 PRAYER

Respond to God in prayer, keeping in mind your reflections from the previous step.

Perhaps you decide to read the psalm again, but this time, imagine that you are writing it. After each line or sentence, pause for a moment and pray with that portion of the text. These pauses might take time, but they are the most fruitful part of this prayer.

Try rewriting the psalm in your own words.

If you want, you can write a reflection on this time in prayer. What fruits did it bear? Was your calling made more clear?

4 CONTEMPLATION

Contemplate one idea from this reading for a while.

"O Lord, you have searched me and known me."

5 ACTION

Guided by God's word, resolve to begin a new life of faith.

Given that you recognize God's call in your life, what changes can you make in or about your life going forward?

14
YOU CALLED ME TO CHANGE HISTORY

From the Gospel of Luke 1

In the sixth month the angel Gabriel was sent by God to a town in Galilee called Nazareth, to a virgin engaged to a man whose name was Joseph, of the house of David. The virgin's name was Mary. And he came to her and said, "Greetings, favored one! The Lord is with you." But she was much perplexed by his words and pondered what sort of greeting this might be. The angel said to her, "Do not be afraid, Mary, for you have found favor with God. And now, you will conceive in your womb and bear a son, and you will name him Jesus. He will be great, and will be called the Son of the Most High, and the Lord God will give to him the throne of his ancestor David. He will reign over the house of Jacob forever, and of his kingdom there will be no end." Mary said to the angel, "How can this be, since I am a virgin?" The angel said to her, "The Holy Spirit will come upon you, and the power of the Most High will overshadow you; therefore the child to be born will be holy; he will be called Son of God. And now, your relative Elizabeth in her old age has also conceived a son; and this is the sixth month for her who was said to be barren. For nothing will be impossible with God." Then Mary said, "Here am I, the servant of the Lord; let it be with me according to your word." Then the angel departed from her.

1 READING

After reading the passage once, read it a few more times.

God calls people to fulfill a mission. He does this without regard for a person's specific situation in order to achieve the results that he, in his infinite wisdom, has planned for humanity. A call, even the simplest one, always has an impact on all of humankind.

In this reading, the angel appears to Mary and proclaims God's plan for her, but Mary is troubled by this news. She is bewildered by what the angel has told her. It is evident that she doesn't yet understand God's plan, and she asks how this can be, because she is a virgin. Mary has every right to ask for an explanation from the angel. The angel explains:

> "The Holy Spirit will come upon you, and the power of the Most High will overshadow you; therefore the child to be born will be holy; he will be called Son of God."

In this verse, we can see Mary's roles in relation to the three divine persons of the Trinity. Mary is the favored child of God the Father, she is the mother of the God the Son, and she is the spouse of the Holy Spirit.

The angel also gives Mary a sign of God's power. Her cousin Elizabeth is with child, even in her old age, "For nothing will be impossible with God." Mary realizes that she is in the presence of a profound mystery, and for this reason she accepts, responding, "Let it be with me according to your word."

2 MEDITATION

Begin this step by considering the following ideas.

In your life as a Christian, do you rejoice in knowing that you are a child of God? Does the message of salvation bring you joy?

In moments when you feel God's call, do you feel troubled or bewildered? Do you also have doubts? What are your doubts? Name them so that you can offer them up to the Lord.

God needs you to acknowledge your doubts and feelings so he can help you overcome your fears.

Do you use God's word in prayer so that he can help you clear up your doubts?

Allow yourself to go beyond reason by entering into God's mystery. Can you understand that nothing is impossible for him? Do you firmly believe this?

Do you allow others who act in the name of God to help you in your discernment? To what extent are you also an "angel," a messenger from God, helping others understand his call?

How available do you make yourself to God's plan? Do you say yes to God's call, even when it implies a change in the plans you have made for yourself already?

3 PRAYER

Respond to God in prayer, keeping in mind your reflections from the previous step.

Holy Father, I give you thanks because you search for me and choose me to proclaim your word. Help me to always hear your call and make myself available to you.

Give me the grace to shape my will, so that my desire leads me to fulfill what you ask of me.

Grant that my life of prayer and service be an example for others to hear and respond to your call.

Thank you for accepting me and choosing me to carry out your mission. I am here to do your will.

Amen.

4 CONTEMPLATION

Contemplate one idea from this reading for a while.

"Do not be afraid! ... For nothing will be impossible with God."

5 ACTION

Guided by God's word, resolve to begin a new life of faith.

I will remain attentive and responsive to God's word.

15

YOU CALLED ME TO HEAR YOUR VOICE

From the Gospel of Matthew 7

"Everyone then who hears these words of mine and acts on them will be like a wise man who built his house on rock. The rain fell, the floods came, and the winds blew and beat on that house, but it did not fall, because it had been founded on rock. And everyone who hears these words of mine and does not act on them will be like a foolish man who built his house on sand. The rain fell, and the floods came, and the winds blew and beat against that house, and it fell—and great was its fall!"

Now when Jesus had finished saying these things, the crowds were astounded at his teaching, for he taught them as one having authority, and not as their scribes.

1 READING

After reading the passage once, read it a few more times.

If there is one calling for the Christian person, in its simplest form, it surely is "listening" to God's word.

In this parable, Jesus teaches us what happens to those who listen to his word. When we talk about listening, we can also imply obeying—that is, we not only hear what is said but also pay close attention and follow through with it.

Listening to God's word informs our daily life. That is why this parable uses the example of two men who built their houses on different foundations, one on sand and the other on rock. In a storm, if a man has built his house on sand, an unstable foundation, the storm will carry it away. If a man builds his house on solid rock, the house will remain after the storm.

In this case, the parable tells us that the man who listens to God's word and builds his life on it will grow without fear of life's storms. But the other, who built his house on shifting, impermanent ground, will need to rebuild after storms and won't find lasting happiness.

2 MEDITATION

Begin this step by considering the following ideas.

How often do you set aside time for prayer with God's word? Do you meditate on it or work to deepen your understanding of it? Do you put it into practice or relate to it?

What is the "sand" on which many people build their lives today? To what extent do you feel your life is built on sandy soil? To what degree have you given in to the things this world offers as happiness?

Are you convinced that God made you to be completely happy? Do you understand that knowing his word and putting it into practice will help you achieve happiness?

Do you accept the word of God as a standard for your life, even if it goes against the trends and expectations of this world?

3 PRAYER

Respond to God in prayer, keeping in mind your reflections from the previous step.

Thank you, Lord, for helping me understand your will, for being so clear with me. I know that I am often confused by the world and all its noise. Help me learn how to hear your word through the clutter that fills the air. Lord, help me build my life on your word and not on my own preferences and personal whims or on those imposed on me by society.

Grant me the faith to build my life on the foundations of prayer and the rock of your word. Lord, I have been afraid of life's storms, but you taught me that I need not fear when my life is built on the foundation of your word.

Help me learn and keep this lifelong lesson.

Amen.

4 CONTEMPLATION

Contemplate one idea from this reading for a while.

> "But [the house] did not fall, because it had been founded on rock."

5 ACTION

Guided by God's word, resolve to begin a new life of faith.

Resolve to base your life on prayer with God's word. Commit to spending time reading God's word daily. This can be accomplished with a meditation app or by dedicating a few minutes every day to read the Bible.

16

YOU CALLED ME TO CHANGE MY LIFE

From the Gospel of Matthew 9

As Jesus was walking along, he saw a man called Matthew sitting at the tax booth; and he said to him, "Follow me." And he got up and followed him.

And as he sat at dinner in the house, many tax collectors and sinners came and were sitting with him and his disciples. When the Pharisees saw this, they said to his disciples, "Why does your teacher eat with tax collectors and sinners?" But when he heard this, he said, "Those who are well have no need of a physician, but those who are sick. Go and learn what this means, 'I desire mercy, not sacrifice.' For I have come to call not the righteous but sinners."

1 READING

After reading the passage once, read it a few more times.

Among the Israelites, tax collectors were some of the most despised people, mainly because they helped the occupying Roman government take money from the people. The Romans were idolatrous, worshiping their currency, stamped with the face of the emperor, whom they considered a god. The tax collectors were considered robbers because much of the money they collected ended up in their own pockets.

However, Jesus saw something in Matthew that others could not. He decided to call Matthew despite the people's reaction and disdain. We don't know what the disciples' first reaction was. Perhaps they didn't understand why Jesus would choose someone like him to be among them. This choice also caused a strong backlash from the Pharisees. But God has his own plans, and he had one for Matthew. Jesus was very clear on this, saying to the Pharisees, "Those who are well have no need of a physician, but those who are sick."

2 MEDITATION

Begin this step by considering the following ideas.

How often do you feel cut off from God because of the decisions you make? When does this lead you to avoid reading his word? Do you feel unworthy or disconnected from God?

This avoidance, self-judgement, and feeling of disconnection are temptations of the devil, who wants to keep you away from God.

Do you accept that God calls you to be a disciple of Jesus despite your weaknesses?

Do you allow your weaknesses to be enough of an obstacle to keep you away from a life in relationship with God? Are you aware of this serious temptation, for which you should be alert and vigilant, and that you should follow Jesus despite your weaknesses?

What would be the "tax collection table" in your life? Is there some position you hold, a role you play, or a practice you keep that you must leave behind to become a true disciple and apostle of Jesus?

Jesus made Matthew, a man whom the Pharisees regarded as impure and a sinner, into a great apostle and evangelist. What can Jesus do with you? Are you willing to put your life in his hands and follow him?

3 PRAYER

Respond to God in prayer, keeping in mind your reflections from the previous step.

Lord, I give you thanks for finding me. You have come into my life. I am, as Matthew was, sitting at a tax collector's table, where everyone can see my sinfulness. However, you come to offer me something new. You come to free me from my sinfulness.

Lord, grant me the strength to get up and leave my own tax collection table. Help me do it with courage.

I hear your voice calling, "Follow me!" But I am afraid, Lord. Help me to conquer my fears; do not let them paralyze me and prevent me from growing closer to you.

Lord, grant that I may know you, and that I may know myself. Because from my life and my lowliness, you want to transform me. I know my past and my faults are of no consequence to you—only my possibilities and my future.

Here I am, Lord, ready to follow you. Show me the way into your light.

Amen.

4 CONTEMPLATION

Contemplate one idea from this reading for a while.

> "Go and learn what this means, 'I desire mercy, not sacrifice.' For I have come to call not the righteous but sinners."

5 ACTION

Guided by God's word, resolve to begin a new life of faith.

Intend to be more attentive in prayer with God's word so that you are able to hear his call. Find the desire to help others to move toward Jesus without fear, because he is the doctor who comes to heal the sick.

17

YOU CALLED ME TO BE FREE

From the Gospel of Matthew 19

Then someone came to him and said, "Teacher, what good deed must I do to have eternal life?" And he said to him, "Why do you ask me about what is good? There is only one who is good. If you wish to enter into life, keep the commandments." He said to him, "Which ones?" And Jesus said, "You shall not murder; You shall not commit adultery; You shall not steal; You shall not bear false witness; Honor your father and mother; also, You shall love your neighbor as yourself." The young man said to him, "I have kept all these; what do I still lack?" Jesus said to him, "If you wish to be perfect, go, sell your possessions, and give the money to the poor, and you will have treasure in heaven; then come, follow me." When the young man heard this word, he went away grieving, for he had many possessions.

1 READING

After reading the passage once, read it a few more times.

In this reading, the young man approaches Jesus and asks him what he must do to receive eternal life, a question that still applies today. Jesus, as Lord and God, gives the answer. In the face of the man's insistence on specific actions, he reminds the young man of the Ten Commandments.

Jesus is the only one who is good, the one God, the one who reminds us of the Ten Commandments. In this passage, he mentions only those commandments that apply to our relationships with other people.

The young Jewish man has always obeyed the commandments. He is a just and good young man according to Moses' Law. So he asks, "What do I still lack? What else must I do?"

This gives Jesus a chance to reveal the new order, which he came to establish. The law makes us righteous, but Jesus replies,

> "If you wish to be perfect, go, sell your possessions, and give the money to the poor, and you will have treasure in heaven; then come, follow me."

This direction saddened the young man, not only because he had great wealth and didn't want to give up his possessions, but also because he knew he was not fully prepared to follow Jesus.

2 MEDITATION

Begin this step by considering the following ideas.

The young man was good. He had good intentions, but his religious commitment was limited. Jesus goes beyond the limits we have for ourselves and asks for perfection.

Is your Christian life limited to times and places where you feel comfortable? How often do you come to Jesus to ask him for help in understanding what it is you still lack?

Do you know that if you go to Jesus and ask him for help, he will tell you what is best for you, even when it is not in line with your own plans? Is your heart open to listen to the truth, or do you want Jesus to support only your own plans?

How willing are you to follow Jesus? Do you want to be his disciple? When you think about material things, relationships, status, and places, what are you willing to give up to follow Jesus?

Not all of our encounters with Jesus will make us immediately happy. If you come to him with your prejudices and superficial desires, and expect Jesus to support those petty plans, you will only find disappointment.

Ask yourself how often you feel sad. Are you desires and motivations leading you to a feeling of sadness and emptiness, or are they leading you to faith and happiness? Is it possible that you have not wanted to follow Jesus fully?

3 PRAYER

Respond to God in prayer, keeping in mind your reflections from the previous step.

Lord, I realize that many times I come to you with my own plans and projects. I realize that they ultimately sadden me. I do not want to go away feeling disappointed after I encounter you.

Help me to obey the commandments and to see clearly the things that get in the way of my encounter with you. Lord, I want to follow you, but I am afraid to leave these things behind. Give me the courage to do your will, to give up the things that get in the way and hold me back from following you.

Amen.

4 CONTEMPLATION

Contemplate one idea from this reading for a while.

Lord, what do I still lack?

5 ACTION

Guided by God's word, resolve to begin a new life of faith.

Resolve to be aware of the things in your life that are blocking a true encounter with Jesus and to remove those that prevent you from following him. Make a list of all these things, and present them to the Lord to be able to start letting go of them. Accept the disciple's journey reverently.

18

YOU CALLED ME TO LEAVE EVERYTHING BEHIND

From the Gospel of Luke 5

Once while Jesus was standing beside the lake of Gennesaret, and the crowd was pressing in on him to hear the word of God, he saw two boats there at the shore of the lake; the fishermen had gone out of them and were washing their nets. He got into one of the boats, the one belonging to Simon, and asked him to put out a little way from the shore. Then he sat down and taught the crowds from the boat. When he had finished speaking, he said to Simon, "Put out into the deep water and let down your nets for a catch." Simon answered, "Master, we have worked all night long but have caught nothing. Yet if you say so, I will let down the nets." When they had done this, they caught so many fish that their nets were beginning to break. So they signaled their partners in the other boat to come and help them. And they came and filled both boats, so that they began to sink. But when Simon Peter saw it, he fell down at Jesus' knees, saying, "Go away from me, Lord, for I am a sinful man!" For he and all who were with him were amazed at the catch of fish that they had taken; and so also were James and John, sons of Zebedee, who were partners with Simon. Then Jesus said to Simon, "Do not be afraid; from now on you will be catching people." When they had brought their boats to shore, they left everything and followed him.

1 READING

After reading the passage once, read it a few more times.

The reading gives an account of a very important encounter between Jesus and Peter, who was still called Simon at the time this story took place. The Scripture doesn't tell us which particular teaching Jesus was sharing at that time, only that he was preaching God's word.

All of a sudden, Jesus asked Peter to navigate his boat into deeper water to fish, even though Peter had fished all night without success. Peter declared that he would obey, not because he wanted to but because the Lord commanded it. Peter's faith was expressed in his work and its results. He obeyed, saying, "Yet if you say so, I will let down the nets."

When they lowered their nets, they caught such a large amount of fish that Peter knew he was in the presence of someone with great power. Afraid and confused, Peter knelt and asked Jesus to leave him, for he was a sinful man. Back then, when a teacher or priest encountered a sinner, he became impure, so Peter had the good intention of not "staining" his teacher. But Peter's teacher could not become stained. On the contrary, Jesus is the one who takes away the sins of the world. He said to the frightened Peter, "Do not be afraid."

Peter and his companions responded to their encounter with Jesus by leaving everything behind and following him from then on.

2 MEDITATION

Begin this step by considering the following ideas.

How do you think Peter felt after this encounter with Jesus?

An encounter with someone that exceeds our expectations can frighten us. What are your fears about encountering Jesus? To what extent can fear paralyze you and leave you sidelined from such an encounter?

Many people don't want to have an encounter with the Lord because they consider themselves sinful, they are afraid, they are ashamed, or they don't want to stain the community. These fears are temptations from God's enemy.

Identify all the things that keep you away from Jesus and present them to the Lord without fear but with the desire for him to receive them, purify them, and invite you to follow him.

3 PRAYER

Respond to God in prayer, keeping in mind your reflections from the previous step.

Like Peter, I too am confused and fearful, Lord. I am so comfortable in my trade, with my boats and my fishing. I am afraid that my sin and my life away from you may harm the community around me and the church. I am afraid that if you enter my life, you may ask me to leave everything behind. These fears are temptations. I can see that clearly now. I understand that you are the only one who can satisfy my thirst for forgiveness and my desire for happiness.

Lord, let me hear again from your lips, "Do not be afraid." Lord, I do not want to give in to fear. I want to follow you. Give me the strength, give me the courage, and above all, give me the decisiveness to leave everything behind and follow you, to be with you forever.

Amen.

4 CONTEMPLATION

Contemplate one idea from this reading for a while.

"Do not be afraid; from now on you will be catching people."

5 ACTION

Guided by God's word, resolve to begin a new life of faith.

Be aware of all the times the enemy of God tempts you to stop following Jesus or to leave him and his church. Place your fears in the hands of the Lord. Find another person who may feel unworthy of following Jesus, and encourage him or her to move closer and embrace Jesus, to trust in his word.

19
YOU CALLED ME TO FORGIVENESS

From the Gospel of Luke 19

He entered Jericho and was passing through it. A man was there named Zacchaeus; he was a chief tax collector and was rich. He was trying to see who Jesus was, but on account of the crowd he could not, because he was short in stature. So he ran ahead and climbed a sycamore tree to see him, because he was going to pass that way. When Jesus came to the place, he looked up and said to him, "Zacchaeus, hurry and come down; for I must stay at your house today." So he hurried down and was happy to welcome him. All who saw it began to grumble and said, "He has gone to be the guest of one who is a sinner." Zacchaeus stood there and said to the Lord, "Look, half of my possessions, Lord, I will give to the poor; and if I have defrauded anyone of anything, I will pay back four times as much." Then Jesus said to him, "Today salvation has come to this house, because he too is a son of Abraham. For the Son of Man came to seek out and to save the lost."

1 READING

After reading the passage once, read it a few more times.

Jesus was known in the region and was passing through the city of Jericho. Zacchaeus was a tax collector, one of a despised group of people. Zacchaeus had heard of Jesus and wanted to see him, and because he was so short, he climbed a tree for a better view.

Jesus, who knows the heart of every person, saw that Zacchaeus had made the effort to climb a tree to see him. Jesus looked upon him with compassion and told Zacchaeus that he would stay at his house that night.

No respectable Jew would dare enter the house of a tax collector, a public sinner. But Jesus did, and caused a great commotion among the Jews. They didn't understand how a respectable teacher would defile himself by entering the house of a sinner.

Zacchaeus's encounter with Jesus was so transforming that he realized that he had many things he didn't need. Because of this, he decided to give half of his possessions to the poor and to obey the law of Moses that one should repay four times as much as one has stolen.

Jesus clearly stated, "Today salvation has come to this house." Obviously, it was Jesus who had entered the house. He was salvation itself. However, in the last verse, Jesus refers to himself as "the Son of Man," who has come to seek and to rescue the lost. In the end, Zacchaeus's call came from Jesus. It was Jesus who sought him, called him, wanted to stay at his house and to forgive him. Zacchaeus accepted Jesus, left his former life behind, and began a new life as a follower of God's word.

2 MEDITATION

Begin this step by considering the following ideas.

What is your desire in seeing Jesus? Do you trully want to find him? What do you expect from your encounter with him?

Zacchaeus had obstacles that prevented him from seeing Jesus. What are the obstacles that prevent you from encountering Jesus? Might one of them be society: what others might say if you did follow him?

How can you overcome these obstacles that prevent you from getting close to the Lord?

Zacchaeus, a sinner, could never have imagined such a personal encounter with Jesus. Do you know that it is the Lord who seeks you out, like Jesus did with Zacchaeus?

Are you happy and joyful when the Lord decides to come closer to you, that is, when he wants to share himself in your life?

When you encounter Jesus through God's word, do you feel there are things in your life that are extra? Perhaps you have accumulated material things and personal relationships out of fear. These things are not necessary. Can you name them and present them to the Lord?

Jesus has come to seek those who are lost. Are you happy to receive Jesus when he comes seeking you?

Think about all the things that you can leave behind. Jesus invites you to begin a new, meaningful life with him. Don't miss this chance!

3 PRAYER

Respond to God in prayer, keeping in mind your reflections from the previous step.

Lord, many people have spoken to me about you. I want to know you.

I have many things in my life preventing me from seeing you, and many things not in keeping with your teachings separating me from you. They are obstacles on my way to you. I have chosen a lukewarm faith: a Christianity that is comfortable and complacent.

I want to overcome these obstacles so that I may know you. I know that your loving eyes are upon me, and I am deeply moved that you call me by my name to come out from where I have been hiding and to be ready to receive you.

Lord, come into my house. Come into my life. Let me always be willing to receive you.

Help me discard the extras that I have accumulated in my heart: my bitterness, my grudges, and the material things I acquired, seeking happiness away from you.

Come and save me. I want to declare and proclaim that, today, salvation has come into my life because you have arrived, and only in you do I find salvation and the fulfillment of life.

Thank you for coming to seek me and redeem me. I offer my life into your hands. Make me your disciple and your missionary.

Amen.

4 CONTEMPLATION

Contemplate one idea from this reading for a while.

"Today salvation has come to this house."

5 ACTION

Guided by God's word, resolve to begin a new life of faith.

Identify an obstacle that separates you from the Lord. Resolve to let go of it.

Give the extra things that clutter your life to someone who may need them more than you. This will make more space for Jesus in your home and in your life.

20
YOU CALLED ME TO PROCLAIM YOUR NAME

From the Gospel of John 1

The next day John again was standing with two of his disciples, and as he watched Jesus walk by, he exclaimed, "Look, here is the Lamb of God!" The two disciples heard him say this, and they followed Jesus. When Jesus turned and saw them following, he said to them, "What are you looking for?" They said to him, "Rabbi" (which translated means Teacher), "where are you staying?" He said to them, "Come and see." They came and saw where he was staying, and they remained with him that day. It was about four o'clock in the afternoon. One of the two who heard John speak and followed him was Andrew, Simon Peter's brother. He first found his brother Simon and said to him, "We have found the Messiah" (which is translated Anointed). He brought Simon to Jesus, who looked at him and said, "You are Simon son of John. You are to be called Cephas" (which is translated Peter).

The next day Jesus decided to go to Galilee. He found Philip and said to him, "Follow me." Now Philip was from Bethsaida, the city of Andrew and Peter. Philip found Nathanael and said to him, "We have found him about whom Moses in the law and also the prophets wrote, Jesus son of Joseph from Nazareth." Nathanael said to him, "Can anything good come out of Nazareth?" Philip said to him, "Come and see." When Jesus saw Nathanael coming toward him, he said of him, "Here is truly an Israelite in whom there is no deceit!" Nathanael asked him, "Where did you get to know me?" Jesus answered, "I saw you under the fig tree before Philip called you." Nathanael replied, "Rabbi, you are the Son of God! You are the King of Israel!" Jesus answered, "Do you believe because I told you that I saw you under the fig tree? You will see greater things than these." And he said to him, "Very truly, I tell you, you will see heaven opened and the angels of God ascending and descending upon the Son of Man."

1 READING

After reading the passage once, read it a few more times.

Here John the Evangelist gives us a series—almost like a chain—of introductions and callings to the Lord:

John the Baptist introduces Jesus as the Lamb of God to Andrew. Andrew goes and finds his brother, Simon Peter, and introduces him to Jesus, declaring that he has found the Messiah, the Christ. Then Jesus finds Philip in that city and asks him to follow him. Philip finds Nathanael, telling him that he has found the one about whom the Old Testament prophesied.

This series of encounters with the Lord shows that whoever encounters Christ always wants to share him with others, so that they too can have an encounter with him.

John the Baptist had followers. Among them was Andrew, the brother of Simon Peter. It was John the Baptist who told his followers that Jesus was the Lamb of God. So they followed Jesus.

Jesus noticed them following him, and asked, "What are you looking for?" They wanted to know where he was staying, and Jesus invited them to follow him. This encounter was so important that they even remembered the time at which they started to follow him: at four o'clock in the afternoon.

Andrew introduced Simon Peter to Jesus and told him that he had found the Messiah. Jesus then gave Simon the name *Peter*, which means "rock."

Later, Jesus found Philip and invited him to follow as well. Philip left everything and followed Jesus. Then it was Philip who sought out Nathanael to introduce him to Jesus. Philip told him that they had found the one whom the Scriptures described, and even though Nathanael questioned where Jesus was from, Philip invited him to join them. Jesus, who reads the depths of people's hearts, addressed Nathanael's doubts by telling him that he was a true Israelite, that there was nothing false in him. Nathanael didn't understand this, so he asked, "How did you get to know me?" Jesus replied, "I saw you under the fig tree." Now, we don't know what Nathanael was doing under the fig tree; we can speculate many things, but it is possible that he was praying. After hearing such an accurate and unexpected response, Nathanael said, "Rabbi, you are the Son of God!" Jesus added, "You will see greater things than these. You will see heaven opened."

2 MEDITATION

Begin this step by considering the following ideas.

Knowing Jesus, or knowing about him, doesn't necessarily translate into a profound encounter with him. It takes more than knowing facts about Jesus as a historical figure to truly know him; we need a deep, prayerful encounter with him.

Who introduced you to Jesus? Was it a friend, someone in your family, a catechist, or one of your teachers? How did you arrive at an encounter with Jesus?

Your encounter with Jesus is the foundation of your faith. Have you allowed Jesus to enter into your life? Do you allow Jesus to guide you? Do you want to lead others to him?

3 PRAYER

Respond to God in prayer, keeping in mind your reflections from the previous step.

Lord, thank you for all the people who have proclaimed your name throughout the past two thousand years. Many have given their lives so that today I can encounter you.

I feel happy and fulfilled by my faith, knowing that you are the Messiah, the Son of God, the one awaited through the ages. You are the beginning and the end. You are the Lord of Life.

Help me make our encounters increasingly frequent and profound. I want to know you, and by knowing you, I want to see myself through the lens of faith, to know myself as I exist in relation to you, Lord.

Lord, many people around me have never encountered you in a profound way. Help me bring them into an encounter with you. Lord, I am also afraid of being rejected. Help me overcome the obstacles that prevent me from speaking openly about my faith. Give me the strength to speak up about you so that others may know you and the joy you bring to my life.

Lord, open my heart to a deeper encounter with you. Help me respond to your call to bring the faith to others, adding more links to the chain of faith.

Amen.

4 CONTEMPLATION

Contemplate one idea from this reading for a while.

"We have found the Messiah."

5 ACTION

Guided by God's word, resolve to begin a new life of faith.

As true believers, we must take God's word into our lives and share it with others.

Resolve to find one person with whom to share your experience of encounter with Jesus, and invite him or her to experience the joy and mystery of encounter with Jesus.

21
YOU CALLED ME TO FOLLOW YOU

From Acts of the Apostles 9

Meanwhile Saul, still breathing threats and murder against the disciples of the Lord, went to the high priest and asked him for letters to the synagogues at Damascus, so that if he found any who belonged to the Way, men or women, he might bring them bound to Jerusalem. Now as he was going along and approaching Damascus, suddenly a light from heaven flashed around him. He fell to the ground and heard a voice saying to him, "Saul, Saul, why do you persecute me?" He asked, "Who are you, Lord?" The reply came, "I am Jesus, whom you are persecuting. But get up and enter the city, and you will be told what you are to do." The men who were traveling with him stood speechless because they heard the voice but saw no one. Saul got up from the ground, and though his eyes were open, he could see nothing; so they led him by the hand and brought him into Damascus. For three days he was without sight, and neither ate nor drank.

Now there was a disciple in Damascus named Ananias. The Lord said to him in a vision, "Ananias." He answered, "Here I am, Lord." The Lord said to him, "Get up and go to the street called Straight, and at the house of Judas look for a man of Tarsus named Saul. At this moment he is praying, and he has seen in a vision a man named Ananias come in and lay his hands on him so that he might regain his sight." But Ananias answered, "Lord,

I have heard from many about this man, how much evil he has done to your saints in Jerusalem; and here he has authority from the chief priests to bind all who invoke your name." But the Lord said to him, "Go, for he is an instrument whom I have chosen to bring my name before Gentiles and kings and before the people of Israel; I myself will show him how much he must suffer for the sake of my name." So Ananias went and entered the house. He laid his hands on Saul and said, "Brother Saul, the Lord Jesus, who appeared to you on your way here, has sent me so that you may regain your sight and be filled with the Holy Spirit." And immediately something like scales fell from his eyes, and his sight was restored. Then he got up and was baptized, and after taking some food, he regained his strength. For several days he was with the disciples in Damascus, and immediately he began to proclaim Jesus in the synagogues, saying, "He is the Son of God."

1 READING

After reading the passage once, read it a few more times.

Saul of Tarsus, a great scholar of the Jewish religion, had been a disciple of great rabbis, among them one by the name of Gamaliel. He was convinced that the knowledge and wisdom he had received from the Old Testament was the truth. To him the followers of Jesus were a threat to that truth. That's why he was so zealous in defending the Jewish faith. He had played a part in the martyrdom of Stephen, the first martyr (see Acts of the Apostles chapter 7), and now he wanted to persecute and imprison all followers of Jesus.

Saul, determined to accomplish his mission, was on his way to Damascus, when a sudden, dazzling light blinded him, and he heard a voice: "Saul, Saul, why do you persecute me?" Jesus is connected to his followers in such a way that when someone does something to one of them, it is the same as if it were done to Jesus himself. Thus, the members of the church are Jesus' body, and Jesus acts in the world through them.

After his encounter with Jesus, Saul arrived in Damascus, blinded. There, Ananias, a saintly man gifted with the ability to hear God's call, accepted the command to go to Saul in the name of Jesus. There he proclaimed the faith, laid hands on him, and prayed for him. After all this, Saul asked to be baptized.

Saul's encounter with Jesus changed him from a persecutor to a follower of Jesus. He was chosen by God to share Jesus' name and message with the entire known world.

2 MEDITATION

Begin this step by considering the following ideas.

As you read and meditate on God's call, remember that you too are called.

Saul fully believed in his Jewish religion, which led to his persecution of Christians and his refusal to encounter Christ. What are your beliefs? Are any of them stopping you from encountering the Lord?

Throughout this series of *lectio divina* exercises, we can see that none of the people who were called was fully prepared to respond to that call immediately. Initially, they made many excuses: "I am old," "I am a stutterer," "I am of unclean lips," "I am a boy," "I am a peasant," "I am a sinner," "I am a man of faith, and I am not going to change the way I practice that faith."

Now, consider the excuses you usually give the Lord. Think about this seriously; you need to truly examine your heart—and yourself—to find the answers.

You may face many obstacles. Even Saul had them, though he later became the great apostle, Paul. Even in his ministry, he never denied these obstacles. Are you waiting to overcome your obstacles in order to commit to follow Jesus? Do not be discouraged—the important thing is a deep desire to follow the Lord, not any obstacle that you must overcome.

The reading also mentions Ananias. He was afraid to go to Saul. Are you perhaps more like Ananias? Do you question the Lord's will for you? Is it time to be an obedient Christian, to change your behaviors and reactions?

When God calls you to act, how often do you question God's plan? Can you turn to prayer in these times?

In Saul, we have an example of how God calls people who might seem the least likely candidates to be his disciples and missionaries. Once he understood the meaning of his encounter with Christ and received the prayer of Ananias, Saul asked to be baptized. This act plunged him into the Trinitarian mystery. From there on, he preached without stopping. We can read about all the great missionary journeys he made throughout his life. Can your commitment and desire to teach others take you from disciple to missionary?

Remember: God sees straight to the heart.

3 PRAYER

Respond to God in prayer, keeping in mind your reflections from the previous step.

Lord, thank you for the lives of the many people who have encountered you and left everything to follow you. Thank you, especially, for the life of St. Paul, the tireless apostle. His example causes me to reflect on my life, Lord. When the church's teachings do not fit my whims, do I battle against the church itself? Sometimes I even feel like Paul did before his conversion: intolerant of those who do not believe as I do.

I ask for forgiveness, Lord. I have not matured enough yet in my conversion.

I ask for your help, Lord. Even if I must fall from my place of pride, as Paul did, and even if my plans are completely changed, I would like to say, "Here am I, Lord; send me!"

I confess that I am afraid. I fear that my plans will have to change, that my intentions will not align with your will. But I understand, Lord, that by staying close to your word, I will find the way to accept your plan and will learn to put my life in your hands.

Lord, grant me the grace to be more like St. Paul, a disciple, an apostle, and a missionary of your word.

Help me leave my pettiness behind, accept your plans of love, and bring others into joyful encounters with you. This is the way to complete happiness.

May I be obedient to your word.

Amen.

4 CONTEMPLATION

Contemplate one idea from this reading for a while.

> "[You are] an instrument whom I have chosen to bring my name before Gentiles and kings and before the people of Israel"

5 ACTION

Guided by God's word, resolve to begin a new life of faith.

Invite your group to carry out a mission to spread the name of Jesus, the Christ, the Messiah and Savior. Discuss a strategy to accomplish this. Where would you start? Whom would you introduce to Jesus? Whom would you prioritize to receive the word of God? Take the initiative as Paul did. Let his example inspire you.

May your journey be blessed as you continue to pray with God's word and proclaim it to others.

ABOUT THE AUTHOR

Ricardo Grzona was born in Mendoza, Argentina. He studied at the Pastoral Theological Institute of CELAM (Medellín), at the Pontifical Gregorian University, and the Salesian Pontifical University (Rome), with an emphasis on evangelization and catechesis. He currently chairs the Fundacion Ramón Pané, which focuses on the formation of parish and diocesan leaders, as well as various church groups.

Also by Ricardo Grzona